CRANBROOK CHURCH OF ENGLAND SCHOOL

These are pictures of the school I attended when I was five years old, about 1915 or 1916, when Miss Sutherland was Headmistress.

I enjoyed this part of my schooldays. Sometimes it was games, other times fun lessons. We did not use paper and pencils very much. We each had a slate and slate pencil, with which we could make a lovely screeching sound. As I moved to higher classes in the school I began to hate it. Perhaps it was because I spent a lot of time at a school in Heathfield due to my mother's poor health. Many was the time I was put on the train at Cranbrook Station bound for Heathfield. I had to change trains at Paddock Wood (I think) and the guard would see that I was on the right train. I must have been about six or seven years old then.

Cranbrook C.E. Primary School in 1985.

It was always a relief to see my grandfather waiting on the platform for me. Coming back to school, the only subjects I enjoyed in the bigger classes were painting and handicraft, usually from the book of Hiawatha, and we made all sorts of things from birch bark, raffia and cane.

Twice a week, we would march through Long Field and across the road to the cricket field. There we had the school allotments on the right hand side of the field, and if a produce turned out a success, we were able to take some home. We did not play a lot of football or cricket, but had to make our own games. These consisted of iron hoops for the boys and wooden hoops for the girls. The iron hoops were driven with a nail into a stick. They were always breaking, but were soon mended at the forge.

Another view of the school, taken from the Ball Field.

Another game was spinning tops. There was a top that you hit with a whip and a peg top called window breakers. A very popular game was rough-riding. Two big boys would have two smaller boys on their backs. The idea was for the smaller boys to grab each other's arms and swing the other round and round. The one that stayed on longest was the winner. Then there was cockles, where you had to stand a card on edge and fling cards at it until it was knocked over, the winner picking up all the cards. There was also flinging cards against a wall and as soon as your card touched those on the ground you had won all the cards and had to pick them up.

Cranbrook school from the Bowling Green end. This has now been pulled down.

SCHOOL HOLIDAYS

Holidays were always looked forward to. There was no television in those days and wireless was in its early stages. We spent hours on the first crystal sets, adjusting the cats whisker and crystal and, if you were in luck, you would get 2.LO of Daventry. The first time I heard music I could enjoy on the wireless was in the house of Mr Ike Hickmott in the Tan Yard. One wall was a mass of coils, condensers and bright omitter valves with batteries under the table. The valves gave so much light it was not necessary to have the oil lamp alight.

A favourite pastime of ours was fishing for newts in the pond at the bottom of Miss Court's garden. In this part of Kent newts were called effits. It was not necessary to use a hook, you just tied a worm onto a piece of string, tied the string to any old stick for a rod and you were away. The newt would grab the worm and nothing would make it let go, it had to be shaken off. The female newt is small and dull brown in colour, but the male is almost twice the size and very colourful with a large zig-zag fin, the length of its back. We were a little scared of the 'Jack' effits, as the males were called. These were supposed to be allied to the legendary Salamander, a lizard-like creature that loved heat and was supposed to live in fire. They are amphibious, just as much at home on land or water. We would also look for frogs' spawn in this pond. We called it frogs' jelly, which we put into a jam jar with pond water and watched the eggs turn into tadpoles. These we would return to the pond.

Collecting birds' eggs was another pastime. If only one egg was taken this did no harm. It was not against the law in those days and my grandson still has my collection. If you found a special egg that had gone bad and did not want to blow it, the best way to get the contents out was to put it in an ants nest — they would eat it out for you. Ants were called ammits in those days.

In the autumn we would go for long walks in the dark looking for glow worms. They were not really worms but insects — Coleopterous (beetles having wings with sheaths). They emit a green glow from the undersides of their bodies. I found the most likely place to find them was between Sissinghurst and Golford, or along the Cranbrook railway line. Tiger nuts could also be found along this line and at the entrance to Cranbrook Cricket Ground, down the lane to White Well. I am unable to find any now because I have forgotten what the foliage looks like. The nuts grow underground and are very sweet to eat.

There was only one swimming pool in Cranbrook, belonging to the Grammar School. When the boys were away on summer holidays we were able to use this, if one could get permission. Sometimes we would get into the pool at night. There was a very high corrugated fence with barbed wire on the top, which made it impossible to climb. But there was a ditch that ran underneath this fence and we small boys could just squeeze through this and get to the pool. The pool was called the Borders, though I never knew why. Mr G. Pope, who lived in a hut close by, looked after the pool for them.

We first learned to swim in a pond on Freight Farm in a pool called the Tench Pond. The farm belonged to Mr Sankster in those days. This pond was half water and half mud. The only stroke we knew was the dog paddle. I can remember the first time I swam across the pond. There was no stopping once you had started as there was about three feet of mud to contend with. We would, whenever we could, swim from late March all through the summer until the frosts came. Harry Collins and George Harrison learned to swim in the old Tench Pond. There was another pond, but this was close to the road and could be seen very easily. Besides, there were cows in the field and one of them chewed the sleeve off my pullover.

The Infants school in winter (1985).

Boys and girls who attended school at Cranbrook. Mr Chapman, Head Master — Cranbrook Senior Boys.
G. Evernden, Maybourne, F.A. Slingsby, ?, F. Nash, J. Dann, E. Holemans, A. Wells, R. Cole, J. Dann, Mansfield, ?, ?, J. Marshall, W. Stone, S. Fisher, R. Couchman. ?, R. Fuller, L. Russell, C. Hones and R. Harris.

Cranbrook Church of England School.
I can recognise some of the boys, but I do not know their first names.
Fuller, A. Slingsby, Osbourne, Dann, Marshall, H. Levett, A. Wells, Mansfield, Nash, C. Hones, J. Elvin, Russell, R. Ratcliff, Fisher, G. Curl and Boniface.

Cranbrook Church of England School.
Weeks, Brown, Marchant, S. Hatcher, S. Neave, V. Farley, F. Dann, H. Parker, C. Hamlin, J. Woodcock, W. Nash, C. Butler, S. Bilsby, D. Milling, A. Tolhurst, J. Watling, A. Dann and B. Lockyer.

Mr Blunt's class. Some of the names:
Miss Wilson, D. Dann, L. Luckford, M. Fisher, E. Bunch, A. Larking, K. Dann, Miss Proert, F. Wainwright, D. Toogood, N. Piper, M. Coleman, B. Elvin, R. Perry, M. White, J. Chapman and L. Lambert.

Some of the boys I can remember:
Osbourne, Farley, W. Parker, Tich Clout,
A. Boniface, R. Wield, Brown, R. Chapman,
Fred Hickmott, Bromley, E. Stone, G. Elvin
and Frank Hickmott.

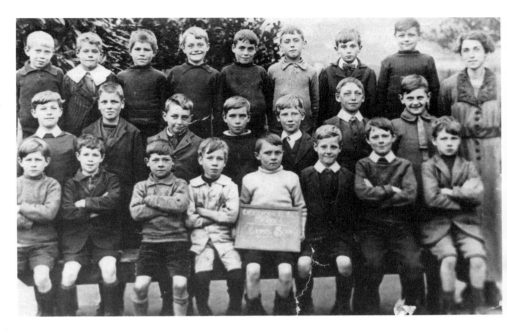

Some of the Boys School Football Team:
Penfold, ?, Osbourn, R. Orpin, Jim Catt,
P. Worsley, Sammy Redhead and W. Hayward.

Some of the teachers after I left school.
Mr Pope, Mr George, Mr Phillips, Mrs Carpenter, Miss Chapman, Mr Croucher and Mrs
Relf.

4

1923. Some of the boys I knew
R. Chapman, W. Butler, A. Boniface, Frank Hickmott, G. Harrison, Mr Blunt, Neave, Osbourne, Wells, Stone, G. Elvin, T. Clout and Chapman.

I think this was a school play. I can name a few of the girls.
L. Tye, Coleman, E. Parker, Kath Dann, V. Tye, Bangham, Elvin, L. Wells, E. Butler and D. Head.

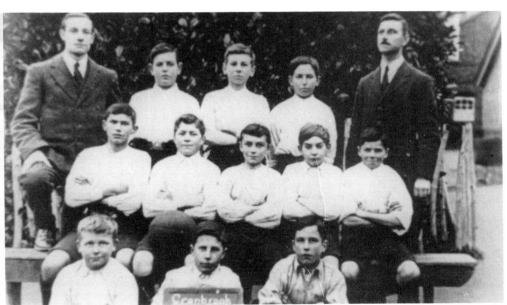

Cranbrook School Senior Boys
I cannot name many of these boys, but I recognise:
Nash, Russell, Elvin, E. Ratcliff, Fuller, Dann, G. Pope, E. Pope and D. Harris.

1940. In Mrs Chapman's class are:
D. Noakes, A. Butler, A. Fryer, I. Fenner,
E. Marshall, B. Humphrey, P. White, H. Tapp,
M. Nash, B. Butler, B. Fryer, S. Hills, A.
Foreman, P. Butler, E. Bennick, E. Barden,
P. Pope and I. Gower.

Cranbrook Senior Girls
I remember a few of these young ladies'
names, but I may have a few wrong:
M. Dann, M. Wells, Saxby, Jarrett, E. Parker,
Bunch and Miss Bangham. (One of Mrs
Chapman's classes.)

1922. I can recognise a few of these faces,
but this was just before my time:
C. Mercer, F. Hinkley, A. Bangham, E. Collins,
Orpin, Mercer, Worsley, Russell, G. Pope,
Marchant, Hinkley, Lansdale, J. Elvin,
Dungey, Cayzer, A. Boniface, Jack Luck and
Wally Butler.

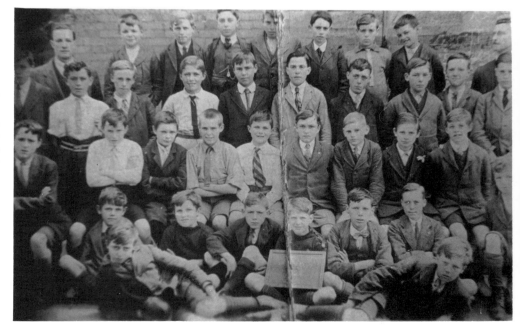

Miss Ransom's class. Early 1920
D. Milling, A. Tolhurst, B. Lockyer, F. Hickmott, J. Marchant, A. Boniface, C. Butler, G. Weeks, J. Woodcock, S. Neave, F. Dann, H. Parker, S. Kazaar, R. Wield, C. Hamlin, V. Curl, G. Standing, Farmer, L. Lambert, L. Wells, M. Metson, J. Chapman, A. Dann, C. Weller, Record and S. Hatcher.

Mrs Chapman's class

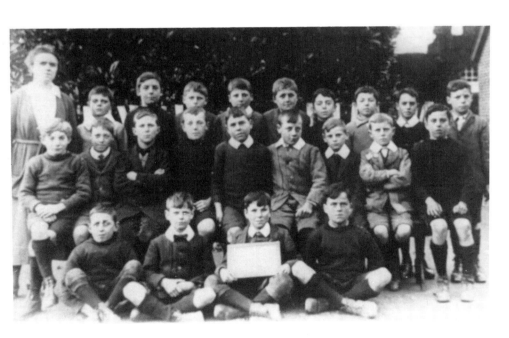

A few more names:
Marchant, E. Collens, A. Bangham, E. Ratcliff, W. Butler, J. Metson, S. Hinkley, G. Hinkley, G. Pope, C. Pethurt, Bilsby and E. Pope.

7

Mr Chapman's class. He came to Cranbrook in 1916 and retired in 1949.

GOING UNDERGROUND FROM THE GAS WORKS TO THE TAN YARD

The Gas holder is the point where the Crane River, as it was always called, comes out in the open after going underground in the Tan Yard. When we were quite small boys two of us decided it would be a good idea to see if it was possible to get from the Gas Works to the Tan Yard. We had an electric torch, which was a novelty in those days, and the batteries did not last so long as they do today. Surface and sewage water terminated in this tunnel. Brick drains ran under the paths in the High Street and Stone Street and also from the Hill and Waterloo Road. All these finished up in the drain.

As we passed under the road we could hear the horses and carts and motors going over the top of us. The tunnel had bends in it and was getting smaller, which made it hard going. Water and sewage was flowing in from all angles. There was also a lot of silt, which made the water deep. By this time we were looking for the end of the tunnel as the torch was getting dim.

The tunnel had now opened up into a large square with a wooden door hanging from the roof by one hinge. We had to move lots of rubbish, old bike frames, pram wheels and wood, but we managed to get out. The tunnel has now been sealed off — just as well really, seeing the state we were in!

Many years ago there was a very large barn-like building on the right hand side of the exit, full of rotting furniture. Mr W. Nash, J.P., owned this old store. This was our favourite playground and we would find all kinds of interesting things there, including old chair and settee springs. These we sold to the upholstery people for sixpence each. This would buy a coconut and we would get twopence change. It would also buy one pound of cooking dates, which were cut from a large block and still had the stones mixed in with them. We could buy ten Woodbine cigarettes for fourpence, or two packets of ten Derbys, or, if we wanted sweets, they would cost three or fourpence a quarter.

Frozen ice-cream was appearing in most sweet shops. This was made in a wooden bucket with a metal interior and a handle on the top. The interior was filled with custard and the handle was swung to and fro like an old-time washing machine. I think the substance they put in the bucket was called freezing salt. Mr Russell, Mr Coughman and Mr Nickles all sold this sort of ice-cream.

Cranbrook School
Featured in the above photograph are:
S. Hickmott, D. Dapson, M. Grigsby, J. Botely, E. Osbourn, P. Russell, J. Stone, S. Larken, E. Ledger, M. Hymers, R. Mercer, T. Wenbourne, E. Dyke, S. Hickmott, M. Fowler, Miss Grigsby, P. Fryer, E. Tapp, S. Croucher, P. Waters and B. Relf.

When the old furniture store was pulled down a large army hut was put up in its place. This became the Cranbrook Picture Palace and the old road leading to it was known as Palace Road. It was sometimes used by travelling theatre groups. I can remember them performing Maria Martin and the Red Barn, East Lyne and many others, which they performed over and over again. Mr Malpass from Forge House was the first person to show 'the flicks' there. Previously they were shown in the Vestry Hall with the projector up in the balcony. All the films in both places were accompanied by a piano. In the Tan Yard Picture House the only heating was a large turtle-type coke stove, and in the winter the public would sit round this. I had a job there when very young, going round with a tray selling sweets. Cadbury's chocolate was elevenpence halfpenny per half pound slab.

Electricity had not yet arrived in Cranbrook, so light and power had to be made with a petrol engine driving a dynamo which produced a D.C. current. I have been informed, by a reliable friend of mine, that electricity came to Cranbrook late in 1926 or 1928.

Stone Street, when the corner shop was Tye and Sons, corn chandlers. Note the large gas lamps outside Freeman Hardy and Willis.

A four in hand outside the George Hotel in Stone Street.

Stone Street in the days of the bicycle, before the cars took over.

LIVING IN COPTHALL COTTAGES DURING AND AFTER THE FIRST WORLD WAR

My first few years in Cranbrook seemed rather primitive. My father was working for the Cranbrook Gas Company, so we lived in one of their cottages. We seldom lived in our sitting room, or front room as it was called. Instead we lived and had our meals in a very small kitchen with no fireplace. The only time we were allowed in the sitting room was on Christmas Day and Boxing Day. There was a big fire in the old inglenook on those days.

My mother was very very houseproud. We were not allowed in the house with our shoes on, we had to take them off in the shed (in those days a shed was more often called a lodge). Normally the only heat we had in our kitchen was a gas light, but when it was very cold we had the gas oven alight. I still have my old slot meter book dated 1924. This was when I emptied gas meters. I see we were one of the best consumers, ours was a penny in the slot meter and had to be emptied twice a quarter. My grandfather was manager of Heathfield Gas Works and lived in a large house in the High Street. My mother was not very happy when she moved to the cottage called Copthall. It was six months before she unpacked her cases!

There was no water over the sink, all water for the three cottages coming from a tap in the yard, which caused a lot of trouble in the winter with the tap freezing. There was only one toilet for the three cottages. There were four people next door, four of us and many more the other side, and it was quite a step to go which could be very embarrassing at times. When we first came to the house, the toilet had twin seats with wooden lids. I think the small one must have been for a child — or learner! There was a purpose wash-house in the yard with a built-in copper. My father would light the fire in this at about six in the morning,

filling the copper and baths with water from the tap in the yard, ready for my mother's wash-day. There was an old mangle in the wash-house which was used by all three families.

Being close to the Gas Works, washing could not be put out to dry until after retorts had been charged with coal. This was at 10 o'clock, 2 o'clock and 6 o'clock and if you had any washing on the lines at these times, they became spotted with soot. You could use the wash-house once or twice a week, but you were expected to keep to your turn. When washdays came round, we knew exactly what our midday meal would be. My father would bake large potatoes on the mouth pieces of the retorts and bring them home with him at 1 o'clock. Apples could be baked like this too, but we always had a large rice pudding made in a large dish. This left my mother free to get on with the washday.

During the First World War, we kept a few chickens, but we did not eat the eggs as they were in great demand. Mrs Fryer would pay sixpence each for our eggs for her dairy. We could get seven buns for sixpence, that was worth more than an egg to us. I do not think these eggs were sold in the shop. I think the baker's name was Mr Lott, who lived two doors from Fryers. At Copthall Cottage there was a small pond. Mr Russell used this to cool the large engine at the mill. Water was pumped up from the pond to the mill, through the engine and back to the pond. In the winter one could see steam coming off the water.

The pond was alive with newts, frogs and frog spawn and it was covered with a green pond weed, until the moorhens found it.

Copthall Cottages have now been modernised, with bathrooms and indoor toilets. The old pond has been filled in and laid to lawn. The big gas engine has been replaced by an electric motor and corn is no longer ground at the mill.

Mr Ernest Hatcher, 4th Battalion, The Buffs, East Kent Regiment.

I think these decorations are for a peace celebration, but it appears earlier than the First World War. It looks like a barrel organ on the right.

This was thought to be a recruiting march to encourage young men to join up.

5th Battalion, The Buffs. Just a few of the people I recognise here are: Mr White, P. Ryon, W. Tapp, T. Williams, G. Burt, F. Hayward, D. Young, S. Barden, G. Gurr, W. Hills, another Barden and C. Burden.

GOING BACK SOME 70 YEARS AGAIN . . .

Mr Dapson, our nextdoor neighbour, worked for Lyle the mineral people, who had their stores in Waterloo Road opposite the old Police Station. He had a horse and a large flat cart to do deliveries in and around Cranbrook, and on certain days he would go to Maidstone to the Lyle Depot to replenish his stock. As a special treat, he would let me go to Maidstone with him. This journey to me seemed to take all day. The highlight of the day was the bottle of pop and biscuits we had on the return journey. Unfortunately for me Mr Dapson moved away, I think to Bowling Green Cottage, which marked the end of my many Maidstone trips. Mr Daniel Reed worked for Wilmshurst the butcher. On Saturday mornings I would go with him in his horse and trap, delivering Sunday joints to all out-lying places.

My father had an allotment and we grew all our own vegetables. For this he required lots of horse manure. As there were lots of horses on the road, we would be sent out with our bodges (you will not find this in any dictionary!) to pick it up. There was much competition for this manure, as we were paid a penny a load. It was called 'Dunging' and brought in quite a bit of pocket money.

You do not see the old rag and bone man these days, but he used to be a regular visitor to the town. His call was 'rag, bottles and bones', but he would take practically anything, old iron, old clothes, jam jars, and always twopence for a rabbit skin. When you think of it, you could buy a rabbit at the door for ninepence or a shilling, this made a good cheap meal cooked with sage and onion stuffing.

Many things have gone for good, such as the old working forge, with its piles of worn-out horse shoes outside the doors and the old round pit also outside the door. This was where the iron tyres for wagons and dung carts were fitted. The tyres were made very hot and two men with sledge hammers forced them onto the wheels. Then a can of water was used to cool the iron: as it cooled the iron would shrink and fit the wheels very tightly.

The sound of hammers striking the anvil was sound never forgotten, nor the smell of the hot shoes being fitted to the horses' hooves. The horses did not seem to mind this a little bit. Then there was Mr Marshall, the snob or boot repairer in Waterloo Road, who would cut out and sew on by hand a pair of soles. He would cut thread, wax it with beeswax and twist boars bristles on each end. He would cut out a pair of soles, then cut a groove all the way round the edge for the stitches to go in, using the awl to make the holes for his thread to go through. Both ends of the thread went through the same hole, but in opposite directions. This job must have taken hours to do. I expect it now takes only a few minutes, but costs very much more.

The way roads are repaired today is a great improvement. The roadmen used to use a tar boiler which was a large tank on wheels with a solid fuel fire underneath and a tall chimney. Forty gallon wooden barrels were used weighing five hundredweight each. These were delivered by horse and cart and thick wooden planks were used to unload them, and again to load the tar into the tank, then the bung was removed to empty them. When the tar was hot, it was drawn off into cans and poured onto the road. Men in clogs would sweep the tar over the road while two other men would use shovels and throw grit over it. A great deal of the tar used came from the Gas Works tar well, pumped up by my father and E. Clout.

11

Cranbrook Church from the east end, showing the old vestry. When I was a choir boy, we used the vestry as a dressing room. Our cassocks and surplices were hung on our own pegs and if they were changed round, we small boys got the blame. Usually, we came out of the vestry singing and in procession straight to the choir stalls. At Christmas and Easter we would have a procession through the middle of the church and back.

Sundays seemed to be taken up with church and Sunday School — church in the morning, Sunday School in the afternoons, church again in the evenings — not forgetting weddings and funerals.

St Dunstans Church

Going down from the Ball Field to the church, on the right you can see a large oak tree. (I think it is called a Turkey Oak.) This was planted in 1862 by Mr John Llyde Allen, Headmaster of Cranbrook Grammar School, to commemorate the marriage of the Prince of Wales, Albert Edward, to the Princess of Denmark.

I do not know how true it is, but I have been given to understand that when the church was built, the field it was built on was flat, but because so many burials have taken place, banks have formed each side of the paths. I was once told by a reliable person that it was around 40,000. This was supposed to be official.

There was a tale going round many years ago that a lot of boys were playing on the church tower and one was supposed to have fallen over the side. Because he was wearing an old fashioned smock it opened out like a parachute and he landed almost unhurt.

When we were very young and in the choir, after practice we would play 'Jack, Jack show your light'. One boy with a torch would hide amongst the tombstones and someone would call out 'Jack, Jack show your light', and the boy with the torch would flash the torch on and off and run to the next tombstone. The boy who caught the one with the torch took a turn with the light. The Police soon put a stop to this game. It was one way of getting warm after the cold church on a dark winter's night.

Just outside the vestry door on the left, there is a grave with a low iron fence round it. The tale was that if you walked round it three times at midnight, the Devil would appear. I never knew anyone who tried this. The low railing with its pointed spikes would not be permitted today. The vestry has been pulled down now and the ground used for cremation burials.

The old oak tree as it was in 1985.

A modern picture of St Dunstan's church in the snow.

Cranbrook Church. This is how I like to remember our church, as it was when I was a choir boy.

Cranbrook Church. I think this was the service when Captain Scott's wife unveiled the memorial to the Alexander Brothers. She was accompanied by the Guards. I should think they are Guards in the back row on the right.

Providence Chapel, Stone Street. This photograph was taken before the Baptismal Pool was built in about 1910 or perhaps a little later.

PROVIDENCE CHAPEL

Apparently there was a chapel somewhere on the Hill in Cranbrook in about 1678 where Mr Huntington occasionally preached. When a division occurred a part of the congregation formed a church at Shepherd's House, High Street in 1780. The late Rev. Beeman was baptised and joined this Church in 1782. In 1795 Mr Beeman, with some others, met in a small building either on the site of the present chapel or adjoining it, where he soon became their leader. About 1800, he had an interview with Mr Huntington, who strongly urged him to preach. This was the commencement of a lasting friendship with Mr Huntington who, after preaching in an old building on Mr Beeman's premises temporarily fitted up, agreed to build the present chapel. This was prepared in London and brought to Cranbrook in horse and wagons. It was erected on the present site and opened by Mr Huntington in 1803. This chapel was erected by voluntary contributions.

This is an old photo taken just below Hill House. On the right can be seen Mercer and Horns workshop. I was told coffins were made there. This building I cannot remember.

The chapel, now the Cramp Institute. The trees were cut down in about 1920 by Mr A. Brown.

This picture was taken from the same place and shows the handcart used when sweeping the roads. The man on the right probably worked in Mr Lott's bakery, just down the bottom of the hill. They used to take buns and cakes round on a tray balanced on their heads. They put a thick round pad inside their hats to protect their heads.

This canopy was used on special occasions and ran from the church to the road. This occasion may have been when Princess Christian came to Cranbrook in 1911.

The occasion of the Coronation of King George V in 1911, showing Mr Fred Winch and Mr F. Marshall. I was told by Mr F. Turner that he was also in this picture with Mr A. Turner and Mr C. Turner.

This picture was taken about 1910 judging by the look of the old car.

Memories 1919-1921

We do not now see the tramps or casuals as they were called, travelling along the roads. These were the people who had no fixed address and would walk from one Union to the next, sometimes called work houses or up the spike. Unmarried mothers would sometimes have to have their babies there if they had nowhere else to go. There were work houses at Tenterden, Cranbrook, Hawkhurst, Ticehurst, Pembury, Battle and many others. The Roaders would do the rounds of these and could be seen hiding their possessions in the hedges or banks and when they left, one could see them retrieving them before going on to the next.

After the tramps had been fed and given a night's lodging, they were expected to pay for this by doing odd jobs about the place. They would often knock at your door asking for hot water to make tea. Most people would make them a can of tea and, if you could, offer them something to eat. They knew all this and were most grateful. It was always said if you gave to them they left some kind of mark behind to let their mates know it was a good house.

Something never seen now, in fact it would be impossible, is a custom when people were sick. If a person was very ill a six inch layer of straw was laid outside on the road in front of the house to deaden the noise of the horses and carts going by. You never heard any shouting when the straw was down. This made an awful mess if the wind got up. Cars would cut out their engines if possible, but there were not many of these.

Winters years ago were a time for snow and ice, you could almost guarantee very deep snow and weeks of ice-skating. The wooden snow ploughs were kept busy for weeks. All the spare time we could get was spent with our toboggans. The best place to go was the old Dairy in Angley Park, this was a long run, starting from the top of the hill at the back of the Dairy and down the steep slope. If you could get past the two oak trees halfway down, you had a long ride to the bottom and through the gate.

Each shop keeper kept his own little bit of frontage clear and if they were unable to do this there were lots of men out of work who would volunteer. Lots of money could be earned clearing footpaths and drives. Winch lake at Bakers Cross has seen many skating parties. The whole lake was illuminated by hundreds of candles in jam jars. The ladies were very good skaters, especially Mrs Harris and Miss Cathy Winch. Most of the ladies used fur muffs but we were not allowed on the ice when the parties were in progress.

'E' Company 23 Kent Home Guard

'E' Company 23 Kent Home Guard
1st row: E.W. Holemans, C. Burgess, V.S. Eves, E. Ratcliff, B.E. Hodges, J.V. Crowcher, R. Gower.
2nd row: T.A.W. Slingsby, D. Marshall, W. Piper, G.E. Luck, U.R. Gianetti, C.R. Scott, H. Tutt, Major H.F. Saunders, R.J.C. Moxham, J. Rowe, A.D. Wilson, F.C. Wickham, W. Hills, E.G. Stevens.
3rd row: S.J. Fisher, G. Penfold, G.H.L. Gilbert, E.E. Tye, J.W. Payne, H. Levett, J.H. Harrison, M.T. Brown, H.C. Hatcher, S.C. Potter, S.T. Stevenson, E.C. Cooms, W. Fedarb, E.C. Robinson, W.J. Brakefield, E. Sands, F.E. Mercer, G.H. Evernden, V.C. Bennett, A. Connally, N. Burr, W.C. Wickham, D.I.C. Fisher, R.G. Draper, F.W. Gower, A.W. Larkin, E. Gower, T.H. Avery, A.F.C. Courtman.
Back row: H.E. Strover, E. Petty, D. Pain, W.A. Kirton, F.W. Love, F. Hayward, W. Brames-Hall, S. Dann, R.E. Levett, F. Worsley, W.J. Penfold, F. Bryant, R.F. Barnes, A.J. Parker, M. Enfield, J.M. Waters, F. Farley, H. Enfield, L.F. Rawlins, H. Jones, J.R. Bourne, P.J. Chapman, H. Parker, F.W. Larken, E. Daw, C. Evernden, J. Dann, A.F. Witt, A.J. Stevens, C.A. Paull, A. Tester, E.T. Mepstead.

Some of the Members of the First World War Homeguard:
Mr Franklin, Mr White, Mr Salmon, Mr Baker, Mr Williams, F. Piper, Mr A. Levett, A. Baker, T. Buckton, two of the Farley brothers, S. Bridgeland, Mr Tye, H. Rummens, Mr Barden (painter), Mr Pethurst, Mr Chapman (School Master), A. Bignall (the Crown), Mr Ratcliffe, Capt Cheeseman, A. Gilbert, R. Hutson and Mr Wells-Hancocks. The boys are F. Head, Hugh Barden, Reg Barden, Les Barden and Ron Evernden.

The unveiling of Cranbrook's War Memorial after the First World War. Could the little girl looking at the camera be a Greengrove?

Angley House and Angley Lake

Angley Lake was another of our favourite sites for skating. This was a large expanse of water not too deep, unless you went to the farthest end of the lake or round the boat house. Between Angley House and the lake, there was a ha-ha. This was a sunken fence put there by Mr Tomlin, owner of Angley Park. He did not want the view from the house to the lake impeded so this fence was built in a ditch. It stopped the cattle from straying but could not be seen from the house.

The thing I remember most about Angley House was the time I had to deliver two soda syphons to the house for Mr Shipman, the chemist. I had been instructed to take these to the back door of the house, but unfortunately for me, or them, there were two bulldogs sitting at the back door and when they started to growl, I decided to go to the front door.

I rang the bell and the butler came to the door, complete with silver tray. After I had explained about the dogs I think he could see I was exhausted following my walk across Long Field with two syphons in a big basket. He asked me to sit down for a while. One of the kitchen staff brought me a glass of lemonade, with real lemon in it, and a few biscuits on a plate. The big house has now been pulled down, but the ha-ha is still there.

These pictures were taken by Rev. Thos. O. Beeman while walking through Angley Woods in 1911. Rev. Beeman called on the little cottage above for a rest.

The photographs were taken at Spratts Bourne, 1911.

I regret this old engraving is the best picture I have of Angley House.

This narrow road was known as Back Lane. It has now become a very busy Cranbrook By-Pass. The house in the picture was Angley Parks West Lodge.

Angley Lake.

Mr Pop Leeves. If there was ice about, you would be almost sure to see Pop making his way to Angley Lake.

The entrance to Angley Woods before New Road came into being, showing Bedlam Stile.

Mill Pond. This was a man-made pond used quite a lot for bathing. Nude bathing put a stop to this and Mr Tomlin had the pond drained.

SHOPS AND PUBS I CAN REMEMBER

Starting from The Hill, The Bridge, left hand side of Stone Street, and High Street

Mr T. Allen, Grocer, The Hill. Serving: Mr Allen, daughter Daisy, Stan Taylor.
Mr A. Gambrill, Old House at Home. Serving: Mr & Mrs and daughter Bessie.
Miss Swatland. Serving: Miss Swatland.
Mr Fryer, Dairy. Serving: Mrs John and Mr Fryer on milk round.
Mrs Bartholomew, Sweet Shop. Serving: Mrs. Sometimes Mrs Santer.
Mr Grey, Bakers. Serving: Miss Grey. Wally and Mr worked in bakery.
Mr Nickles, Sweet Shop, Cigarettes. Serving: Mr and Mrs. Darts in the evenings.

Stone Street

Mr Shipmans, Chemist. Serving: Mr and daughter.
Mr Brown, Furniture Dealer. Serving: Mr and daughter.
Miss Gurr and sister, Fruit Shop. Serving: The two Misses Gurr.
Mr Cayser, Gas and Water Fittings. Serving: Father and sons I think. Not certain.
Mr Trowel, Milkman. Serving: not certain. Boys did milk round on bicycles with a churn in the sidecar.
Mr Elliot, Green Grocer. Serving: Mr and Mrs I think.
Mr Jack Russell, Sweets, Cigs. Serving: Mr. Sometimes his daughter.
Mr Chittenden, Grocer. Serving: Mr and his son Jack. Usually had errand boy.
Mr Jack Waters, News Agents. Serving: Mr Waters and assistants. I did a newspaper round for Mr Waters in 1923. I can just remember the last few names. They were Eke, Thurston, Perkins, Head, Coles, and Cook. I also had to clean the knives in a machine with a pink knife powder, and afterwards scrub down the yard.
Mr William Winch and Sons, Estate Agents. Serving: Mr Winch and assistants.
Mr Wilmshurst, Butcher. Serving: Mr Danial Reed and, I think, Mr T. Hickmott.
Mr Couchman, Sweets & Cigarettes. Serving: Mr and Mrs Couchman.
Mr Springett, Boots & Shoes and a Taxidermist. Serving: Mr and Mrs Springett.
Taxidermist (stuffing animals). Serving: Mr and Mrs Springett.
The Bull Public House. Serving: Mr and Mrs Pope.
Mr Bailey, Music Shop. Serving: Mr Bailey and daughters.
George Hotel, Queen Elizabeth slept here 1573.
Marchant and Tubbs, Clothiers & Outfitters. Serving: Mr and Mrs Smith.
Mr Rumens, Grocers and Provisions, 2 shops. Serving: Mr Rumens, Miss Nash.
Post Office, Telephone Box inside. Serving: Mr Wells, Mr Pearson, Mr Best.
Mr Rolf made Cycles, sold Motor Parts. Serving: Mr Rolf.
W. Nash, J.P., Furniture Dealer. Serving: Mr Nash and son.
Mr W. Smith, Tailor. Serving: Mr Smith.
Mr Leaves, Shoe Repairs. Serving: Mr Leaves.
Mr Bob Barden, Builders, Wall Paper, Paints. Serving: Mr and Mrs Barden.
Mr Varley, Fish and Chips. Serving: Mr Varley and sons.
Mr Hamlin, Fruit Shop, for a short time. Serving: Mr Hamlin (where Mr Sills is now).

Top of the town, coming down left hand side. High Street

Mrs Lansdale, Sweets and Cigarettes. Serving: Mrs Lansdale.
Duke of York Public House. Serving: Mr Revell and Mrs.
Prince of Wales Public House. Serving: Mr Foreman.
The Crown Public House. Serving: Mr Bignell and family.
Mr Beeken, sold Household Goods. Serving: Mr Beeken and family.
Mr Dadson, Bakery. Serving: don't know.
Mr Hougham, Singers Sewing Machine Shop. Serving: Mr and Mrs Hougham.
Mr Pethurst, Fruit Shop (should be 2 doors up). Serving: Mrs Pethurst.
Doc. Shaw, Surgery, High Street. Serving: Doc. Shaw.
Mr Stickles, Photographer. Serving: Mr and Mrs Stickles.

An old print of the White Lion Inn.

PUBS AND SHOPS I CAN REMEMBER WHEN AT SCHOOL

Bangham and Son, Boot Repairs, Musical Instruments. Serving: Mr Bangham and Son.
Powdrill and Sons, Builders Material. Serving: Mr Powdrill and Miss.
Mr Stone, Flowers and Fruit. Serving: Mrs Stone, Mrs Colson.
Charlie Milling, Bicycle Shop. Serving: Mr and Mrs Milling.
Strange, Wireless Shop. Serving: Mr and Mrs Wright.
Miss Jenner, Paper and Book Shop. Serving: Miss Jenner and Miss Barham.
Mr Burnham, Tailor. Serving: Mr Burnham.
Mr Bridgland, Seed Shop. Serving: Mr Bridgland.
Mr Cleovuluspolyryalus or Mr Cleo. Serving: Mr and Mrs Cleo. Mr Cleo made extra long cigarettes on the counter for one penny each. Also sold sweets.
Mr Jones, Fish Shop. Serving: Mr Jones and Bill Stone.
Nash, son of William Nash, Furniture. Serving: Mr Nash.
Mr Glover, Fred Smith, Tanning Skins. Serving: Mrs and Miss Smith.
Mr F. Parker, Baker. Serving: Miss Aunty Parker and Miss Amy.
Jewellers Shop.
Mr Moore, Barber, Hair Cuts 3 pence. Serving: Mr Moore, Mrs Moore in shop.
Palmer and White, Outfitters, Men & Women. Serving: Mr White and shop assistants.
Mr Burgess. In Carriers Road (Tinsmith). Serving: Mr Burgess and Percy.
Mr Salmon, Baker and Teas. Serving: Family.
Mr Rea, Clothes, Outfitters (Stone Street). Serving: Mr and Mrs Rea.
A. King, Barber, Hair Cuts 4 pence. Serving: Mr Moore.
Mrs Wilson, Sweets and Cigarettes. Serving: Family.
Hudson, Chemist. Serving: Mr Hudson and son Ron.
Freeman, Hardy and Willis, Boots and Shoes. Serving: Mr Bent and assistants.
World Stores, Grocers. Serving: Manager and assistants.
Mr Ratcliff, Butchers. Serving: Mr Ratcliff, Ted and Dick. Mrs Ratcliff at the desk.
Mr Rolf, Wireless Parts, Battery Charging, Air Gun Pellets. Serving: Mr Rolf.
Mr Pain, Furniture and Funerals. Serving: Mr and Mrs Pain.
Mr Simmons, Stationers and Printing. Serving: Mr Simmons, two daughters.
Finnimores, Ironmonger. Serving: Mr Finnimore and assistants.
International Stores, Grocers. Serving: Manager, Miss Smith, Miss Brown, Ron Evernden.
Stokes and Sons, Outfitters & Hatters. Serving: Stokes and assistants. I think.
Hocken, Milkman. Serving: Mr and Mrs Hocken.
Noahs Ark, One time Fish and Chips. Serving: don't know.
Fred Curl, Paraffin (Waterloo Road). Serving: Mr and Mrs Curl.
Mr Marshall, Boot Repairs. Serving: Mr Marshall.
Mr W. Rivers, Forge, Shoeing Horses (The Bridge). Serving: Bill Rivers.
George Nickles, Cigarettes and Sweets. Serving: Mr and Mrs Nickles.
Coffee Tavern, Tea and Coffee. Serving: Mr and Mrs Edwards.

Mr Simmons lived at this shop with his two daughters. He was a printer by trade.

19

An old photo of the White Lion Inn, now the International Stores, also showing Mr W. Nash's furniture shop and Mercer and Horns building premises. Both of these buildings have now been pulled down to make way for the Co-op.

A.Wells, Miss Brown, Mr Carter, Miss Smith and R. Evernden outside the International Stores when it was in Stone Street.

An early photograph of the International Stores. I am unable to recognise any of these people but it was when gas lamps were used for lighting.

Stone Street, showing the old clock that was there for many years. Rumour has it that it went to Tenterden. Mr Trowel had a milk churn fixed to the bicycle in the picture.

An unusual view of the Market Cross taken from the church steps, also showing the Bull Hotel, now Cranbrook Engineering. The George Hotel had large stables at the back and one could telephone from there. Marchant and Tubb next door sold clothing and footwear.

This picture shows three houses being pulled down to make way for the Lipton Stores.

Looking up the street just below High House. There was a little shop on the other side of the road.

T.S. Stokes and Sons was a very large drapers premises, with a small hat factory at the rear.

Hop Picking in Cranbrook

Hop picking was a very exciting time for us children, lasting six to eight weeks. The shops did a lot more trade and all the pubs were overflowing every night. We had to get up very early, usually in the dark, and walk about 1½ miles to Coursehorn Farm and then there was another long walk to the hop gardens. When we were picking in the Folly Gardens we would sometimes get a ride in the farm wagon. We had to carry macs, food, boxes and umbrellas; the umbrellas we used to put the hops in. We used the tap at the farm for water. Sometimes, when it was very cold, we would pick up faggots from the farm and make bonfires between the bins.

Mr Smith, who owned the hop gardens, with his daughter Olive, now Mrs F. Piper of Church Cottage. I think the boy on the left was Mr Smith's son.

Mr Bakers picking hops. Some bins were divided down the middle as this one is and known as half-bins. His son, Albert, was a Kent Messenger reporter and lived at Dearn Villa.

Glassenbury oxen with a load of pokes.

Sissy Clayton, Mrs Osborne, Bert Osborne and Emily Fread are shown here.

At about 10 o'clock we would stop for lunch and at 12 o'clock the 'pole puller' would call 'ALL TO DINNER'. By this time the kettle would be boiling on the fire. We would lay pokes on the bins to sit on and the tea was dished out. You had your own cup and helped yourself from the can. The tea was very strong with lots of condensed milk in it, then out came the food, nearly always bread and cheese, cake and a few apples. The 'pole puller' would now call 'all to work' depending on how many hops were required by the oast. The pole puller was so called because in the early days the hops grew up poles and it was his job to pull them up. I do not know why, but the food always tasted better in the open. With your fingers black with hop stain, it gave the food a bitter taste and seemed to improve the flavour. We children were given a set number of boxes to pick, after that we were free to play or go mushrooming or nutting.

About 4 or 5 o'clock they would call 'pull no more bines tonight!'. My father worked for the Gas Works as a stoker, and when on nightwork, he would come out and give us a hand. He always brought us sweets or fruit and gave us a ride home on the crossbar of his cycle. We always had a cooked meal when we got home; this was usually fried potatoes and runner beans. There were three sorts of pickers — the Londoners went to the hopper huts, the home pickers went home at night and the strangers went to the caravans and tents.

There was a lot of competition to get the best hops. Everyone would walk round the gardens in their dinner hour to see where the next set was going into, if there were good hops. There were lots of dodges going on, including cutting the bines and putting them in the bins, or if the hops were poor, they would start a fight or climb up on the wires, anything to cause a delay.

The Smith and Evernden family. This little hop garden was called Smith's Gardens and was situated behind the little chapel at the St David's Bridge Road. There were three cottages in front of this garden. Mrs Moore lived in No. 1, Mr Smith in No. 2 and Mr Williams and Mr 'Happy' Beeken in No. 3. Mr Smith owned the gardens. The cottages have now been pulled down. You can see the hops growing up the poles. The hops were measured in bushel baskets. In those days you had to pick six, seven or even eight bushels for a shilling. This was called the 'Tally'.

Before people could read or write, they used sticks to keep count. Notches were cut into each side of the stick, then the stick was split down the middle and each had a piece and when paid out the stick had to 'Tally'.

This photograph shows Albert Butler, Nellie Butler, Kate Faulkner, Vic Russell, Daisy Chapman and Mrs R. Russell.

Measuring the hops into the pokes, these were supposed to hold ten bushels.

Great Swifts House and Park

Unfortunately, this lovely house has been pulled down and the site rebuilt upon. When we were small children, we had great times in and around Great Swifts. I will always remember our Sunday School treats, sitting along the driveways with our mugs of tea and plates of Mr Parker's cakes and sandwiches. We had all kinds of races and games of every description. We all seemed to get a small prize.

When we were a little older we played in the woods of the house. According to Mr Catt (I think he was the keeper or bailiff) the woods were strictly private, but this did not stop us exploring. There was a deserted farm house with lots of old buildings in the woods. A kind of wild chicken could be seen about the old buildings — they were able to fly quite well and were using the sheds to nest in. They looked very much like game birds to me. The house was supposed to be haunted — in fact we called it the 'Haunted House'. Some years later Elizabeth Taylor lived in this house with her mother, I think it was when Captain V. Gaslet owned the Great Swifts.

Another place we loved to explore was round the Lake Chad area. This lake is an exact replica of Lake Chad in Central Africa, complete with native thatched huts on the island, and other land marks. It was discovered by Claud and Boyde Alexander the explorers and the lake on Great Swifts land is a memorial to them. In Cranbrook Church there is another memorial to them, situated on the right side of the west doors. I am told by a friend that this was unveiled by Captain Scott's wife, mother of Peter Scott,

The funeral of Col. Alexander of Great Swifts Park, 22nd August 1917.

the famous wildlife celebrity. Of the four brothers, Claud died in Africa, 1904 in Mofoni. Boyde was killed in Africa, 1910 in Nyeri. Herbert lived in Willesley House and Robin in Great Swifts. Col. Alexander was their father. He died in August 1917 and was taken to Cranbrook Church in one of his farm wagons, followed by one of his two sons. In those days when there was a funeral and the cortege was passing by, all shops would be closed and blinds drawn, as they were in private houses, and almost all men in the street would stand still and remove their hats to show their respect.

Another postcard of Col. Alexander's funeral.

Great Swifts House and the boat used by Claud and Boyde Alexander on Lake Chad in Africa.

Great Swifts Old World Fair, 1922. Some of the people present were Sis Oyler, Kath Dann, Mrs Doderall, E. Bunch and Miss or Mrs Turner.

Members of the Bincough Sword Dancing Group are: ?, Ted Hickson, ?, ?, Vic Allen, Lionel Baker, Claud Bunch, ?, Daisy Marshall, Taylor, Winnie Baker, Nellie Fread, M. Grover, Phyllis Taylor, Daisy Allen and Winnie Kemp.

Darby and Joan Tea Party — some of the people I can remember here are:
Helpers: Mrs Clark, Ellie Parker, Miss Joyce and Members: Mr Jack Diamond, Mrs Dapson, Percy ?, Shrimp Thatcher, Mr & Mrs Kirton, Mr Collens, Mrs A. Woodcock, Mr & Mrs Neve and Mr Weeks.

Early 1900. The carrier's cart could be from Hawkhurst and the man's name Mr Lockyer, but I am not sure.

An old photo of the High Street with steps and a ramp going from the pavement out into the road. Note the old gas lamp with upright mantle.

The top of the town looking down the street. The cottage near the man with his dog was burnt down and Opher Villa built on the site.

Mrs Pethurst has a very old Cranbrook family name. The house with the two bay windows was a fruit shop where Mrs Pethurst raised her family. There was a little shop nextdoor run by a Mr Beeken. The shop came to the edge of the path, but has now been pulled down.

Mill pond.

Back Lane, as it was called before it became Cranbrook By-Pass.

Two general views of the High Street.

The old Post Office when the phone was inside in a soundproof box. When I was 14 years old I had to use this a lot as the Gas Co. had no phone. You had to ask the operator to get the number for you as there was no dialling. Mr Rolf had a cycle shop and a garage next door when he made his own cycles.

The High Street when Princess Christian
visited Cranbrook in 1911.

The Coronation of George V. The house
behind the tree, now Bell House, was used as
a recruiting depot in the First World War.

This is the entrance to the Fire Station. The
street was decorated because of a visit by
Princess Christian in 1906.

Lloyds Bank in the High Street. This building, although much admired, is only mock Tudor. When we came to live in the High Street the house was called Woodside and looked like the picture below. I am told that Joe Brown did most of the carpentry on the front. He lived in the old house next to Shipmans, the Chemist.

Woodside as it was 60 years ago. Dr Wood lived here for many years and his daughter, Alice Wood, after him.

The school taken from the church gate in winter (1985).

An earlier Bedlam Stile.

This is what Winchs Lake looked like when first made. You can see the old brewery and the tall chimney, also Bakers Cross House, home of William Winch.

John Russell, Union Mill, Cranbrook

Mr Russell was a very experienced engineer and did all his own repairs to the huge gas engines at the mill. He was also engineer to the Cranbrook Gas Co. All the new engines at the works were fitted by him and his assistant, Charlie Poole. J. Russell and an old chap named Colonel Baker would paint the whole of the mill using a ladder and two cradle ladders to hang over the side of the cap. Colonel Baker would not go on the cap unless he had consumed two or three pints of beer. The sweeps were removed for painting and put on trestles in the field. The old sweeps had a twist in them. Mr Baker had a brother who lived down Chittendens Alley and repaired shoes.

M.J. Russell, using his long ladders and cradle ladders for painting the mill, can be seen crawling along the top. One of the Cranbrook Gas Co. gas holders stands in front of the mill.

This is where the River Crane reappears after going underground.

John Russell had two brothers (Paul in the centre and Phillip on the right). The little girl in the front is Helen West. Paul served in the mill and when we were small we had to go there for chicken feed. Occasionally he would give us a square dog biscuit, which were very hard but we loved them. Sometimes if he was in a good mood he would give us a handful of Lotus bean pods. They were very sweet and hard, brown in colour with very hard red beans inside. Phil I do not know much about except that he was an artist and an old-time dancer.

Mr T. Terry and family with his pony and trap. They were chimney sweeps and lived in Tippins Close. They had a big pit in their garden to store the soot.

Mr George Parker Smith, part-time postman in his uniform.

A very early photo of Mr T. Allen's shop. I think Mr S. Allen was his father.

Mr William Smith and Mrs Minnie Smith, mother and father of Elsie, Ireni and William Frederic. Miss E. Smith still lives at 35 High Street. The ramp outside Miss Smith's house was so that a Mr Pankhurst could take his horses from the road on to the path and up the passage to the back of his house.

The Parker family. Harry, Chris, H. Parker, Frank, Amy, Freda, Mr and Mrs Parker, Minni, Ella and William.

The Parker family on the occasion of Herbert Parker's 21st Birthday party.

A lesson in string music — I think this was at St Lawrence School in the High Street. Mr Albert Baker is on the cello, one of the young ladies was Miss Turner, now Mrs Hook.

Cranbrook Football Team.
T. Tapp, B. Hodges, C. Moaks, R. Dapson,
one of the White boys and his brother Peter,
E. Sharman, S. Hickmott, A. Bilsby, R. Coleson, P. Smith, T. Tapp, G. Silk and Mr Rivers.

The Cranbrook 1920 Football Team
Jim Bottle, B. Potter, J. Couchman, B. Vine,
A. Gilbert, G. Bignall, Mr Brew, ?, L. Baker,
?, Parks, Bob Barden and Sacker Barden.

An old Cranbrook football team, 1908-1909.
The only one I recognise is a Mr I. Hickmott,
from the Tan Yard.

Members of the Cranbrook Wednesday Cricket Club
S. Green, Mr Smith, Bridgeland, E. Stone, E. Ratcliffe, E. Coughman, Jones, Pop Leaves, S. Butler and W. Hayward.

This photograph was taken in 1947 and shows J. Pearce, J. Tappenden, R. Bringlow, G. Mercer, K. Humphreys, Mr Cawthorne, Sam Dann, Mr Eldridge, Mrs Bryant, G. Manktilow, F. Bryant, Mr Price, R. Bourne, Mrs Smith, W. Rivers and Mr Hodges.

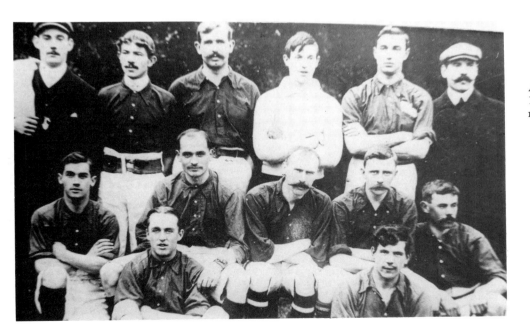

Another old Cranbrook football team, early 1900s. Mr A. Gilbert is the only one I recognise, third back row.

Cranbrook Bowls Club. Shown are:
Mr T. Allen, Mr Springet, Mr & Mrs Wield,
A. King, Mrs King, Mrs Court, Mr Alexander,
Mr Moore, Miss Parker, Mr Parker, Rev.
Swingler, Mr Ratcliff, Mr A Baker and Laurie
Taylor.

Cranbrook Bowling Club
Anty Parker, Mrs Parker, T. Allen, Mr Parker,
Mrs Clarke, Mr White, A. King, A. Roe,
R. Parsons, Mr Moore, J. Russell, Maj. Clarke,
Mr Simmons, D. Ratcliffe, Mr Burgess and
Mr Ratcliffe.

Willesley Billiard Club, about 1928
Back row: C. Hones, G. Leaves, A. Boniface,
E. Holemans, J. Clout, H. Woodcock and
J. Hones.
Bottom row: B. Leaves, S. Readhead, Pop
Leaves, Mr Alexander, C. Butler, E. Stone
and Mr Hones.

Rescue and Red Cross:
W. Rivers, F. Powdrill, N. Little, M. Welstead, Curate, E. Bartholomew, S. Wersley, A. Dann, G. Curl, T. Turner, P. Woodgate, F. Parker, Mr H. Parker, Col. Toke, H. Woodgate, S. Norman and Sid Curl.

Some of the Girls' Friendly Society at Tenterden are: Miss Eldridge, M. Dann, S. Monkton, A. Hall, J. Bryant, E. Dann, S. Rolfe, C. Baker and J. Poole. They performed at the Royal Albert Hall in 1939.

Cranbrook C.O.D.'s.
Some of the faces I recognise are: Mrs Lea, P. Russell, F. Hones, W. Goddard, Mrs Wilks, I. Wilks and wife, Mrs Green, Miss Hayward, Miss Cheater, Mrs Nash, Brenda Fryer, Mrs Allen and daughters, V. Cawthorn, Mrs Banfield, Miss Allsford, P. Bridger, Mrs Draper, Mr Ives, Mr Banfield, Mr Clarke and Mrs Clarke.

Tom Tapp's Wedding. T. Tapp and his wife, with his mother and father, the three Bunch sisters, Mr R. Chapman and brother-in-law, T. Tapp and a Mr Fisher.

Mr & Mrs A. Butler's Golden Wedding. The family are: Victor, Ernest, Fred, Alfred, Charlie, George and Jack. Miss Cath, Mr A. Butler, Mrs Butler and Nell. Albert, Sidney and Arthur (not in picture). All 10 boys were in the First World War.

Back row: E. Stone, L. Neave, S. Bilsby, E. Dann and G. Elvin.
Front row: Head G. Harrison, Chapman, E. Butler, H. Parker and D. Hayward.

Taken during the First World War, this photograph shows William Charlie Hickmott, better known as 'Topper', a name inherited from his father. Apparently, the old chap was a very good gardener and took many of the top prizes in the garden shows, hence the name 'Topper'. They were a well-known Cranbrook family and lived in the Tan Yard on the bank for many years. They were a very large family but unfortunately Mrs Hickmott died when the family were quite young. There was Lily, Gladys, Charlie, Alfie, Derrick and Reg. Mrs Hickmott can be seen in the top right hand corner.

Mr Hickmott worked for Mr Wilks, a butcher in Stone Street for 28 years.

Lily, Gladys, Charlie and Alfie Hickmott, taken about 1928.

Mr & Mrs Hatcher, Harry Hatcher's father and mother.

Mr & Mrs Blackman from Swattenden, with their family, which included twins. Mr Blackman worked at the brewery for some time.

Mrs Smith, Riverdale, High Street on her 90th Birthday. (Photo by Mrs L. Gower, her grand-daughter.)

Hugh Barden, the Rev. Bradshaw and Peter Coleman.

The old Police Station in Waterloo Road. There was an office, two dwelling houses and the cells. All this has since been pulled down. It is now a kitchen and dining room for the Grammar School.

Waterloo Road. This is the bottom of Windmill Hill before the houses on the left hand side of the road were built. The area was a hayfield when this photograph was taken.

Glassenbury House. This was the home of the Roberts family. Miss Jane Roberts married Baron Nicolaus Von Nettelbladt. The house was surrounded by a moat with a bridge in front of the house. Napoleon's horse, Jaffer, is said to be buried in the grounds.

Cranbrook Post Office Engineers celebrating the promotion of one of their colleagues, Mr Milton. Some of the people present are: R. Coleson, J. Foster, Mr R. Coleman, Mr Evans, F. Collins, C. Russell, Mr Wyatt and Ben Grounds.

Presenting the Colours in Rammel Field are Col. Alexander and, I think, Capt C. Winch, also Pat Ryan.

Miss Hills of the World War One Land Army.

Mr Albert Baker of Dearn Villa, Kent Messenger reporter.

Mrs Nellie Hickmott from old Bank Street, selling flags.

My wife Jane and daughter Ann. Ann has nine grandchildren now.

CRANBROOK PARISH COUNCIL.

FIRE ENGINE ESTABLISHMENT.

EDWIN PAINE (*Superintendent*).
WALTER MOORE (*Deputy-Superintendent*).

G. CRUMP, G. BUTLER, A. BUTLER, E. STONE, F. CURL, G. F. HINKLEY, F. BUTLER,
T. HICKMOTT, J. SAXBY, W. NEVE (*Firemen*).

REGULATIONS.

1.—When the Engines are called out, each man to repair to the Engine House with all possible speed, a proportionate deduction will be made from the pay of those not reaching the Fire as soon as the Engine.

2.—The Engines are not to be taken to any Fire *out of the Parish, unless ordered or sent for by some responsible person,* and in no case to be taken out without a sufficient number of Firemen in charge.

3.—The Engines, and the men, are to be under the entire control and direction of the Superintendent and, in his absence, of the Deputy, no strangers are to be allowed to ride on the Engines, or in any way to interfere in their management.

4.—The Superintendent to be allowed to employ in addition to the Firemen, any number of men that may be **NECESSARY FOR WORKING THE ENGINES.** Such men shall be paid at a rate per hour to be arranged by the Superintendent.

No Beer, or other Refreshments to be paid for, except such as may be thought necessary and be ordered by the Superintendent for the Firemen and extra men authorised to be employed.

5.—The Superintendent, or Deputy in charge, shall, immediately after every Fire, furnish the Parish Council with an account of the whole of the expenses incurred, a list of the men who were employed, and a receipt signed by every man employed for all money paid to him. The Council decline to accept any liability for any payment made unless this regulation is strictly observed.

6.—Whenever an Engine shall be sent for out of the parish, the sum of £2 shall be charged therefor, and the person sending for it shall pay all expenses.

7.—The Salary of the Superintendent for keeping the two Engines and appliances at Cranbrook in good condition, shall be £6 per annum payable half-yearly.

8.—The Superintendent shall report to the Council at once any vacancies occurring in the Brigade.

9.—The Superintendent shall also make written Reports to the Council :

(*a*) A Report as to the condition of the Engines, Hydrants, and all fire appliances after each drill and shall include in such Report the names of the Firemen attending such practice and his remarks as to their efficiency, and the nature of the work performed at each drill.

(*b*) An Annual Report in writing to the Council embodying the details of the Quarterly Reports, a statement as to attendance and efficiency or otherwise of each Fireman in the Brigade, the number of calls in the year, the number of Fires in each year with details thereof, a certificate as to the condition of the Engines and all Fire appliances, suggestions for the improvement and general efficiency of the Brigade and any other matters he may be directed by the Council to add to such Report.

The Annual Report is to be furnished to the Clerk to the Council on 1st May in each year.

10.—All Members on joining the Brigade shall sign a stamped agreement to deliver up Uniform and all Accoutrements when they leave the Brigade.

PAYMENT OF SUPERINTENDENT AND FIREMEN.

	SUPERIN-TENDENT.	DEPUTY.	FIREMEN.
	s. d.	s. d.	s. d.
For attendance at the Engine House when Fire Alarm sounded and not sent out, until dismissed by Superintendent, per hour	5 0	2 6	2 0
When an Engine goes to a Fire and not used or detained or when an Engine is actually used or detained, per hour	6 0	3 0	2 6
For every hour when attending Fires out of Cranbrook Parish	7 0	3 6	3 0

The Deputy Superintendent when in charge of Engine shall be paid the same as the Superintendent.

The Engines, Hydrants, and Fire appliances to be tried every other month, when 2/- will be allowed to each fireman present, Deputy Superintendent 2/6, Superintendent 5/-.

Keys of the Engine House are kept by the Superintendent, Deputy Superintendent, Firemen and also at the Post Office.

GEO. A. CALCUTT,
Chairman of the Cranbrook Parish Council.

1923.

The regulations for Cranbrook's 'Fire Engine Establishment' as laid down by Cranbrook Parish Council in 1923.

The Cranbrook Cup-Winning Football Team
Col. Alexander, W. Cooper, W. Carden, D. Parks, J. Coughman, E. Bayfield, Sergeant Potter, J. Bottle, C. Stanbridge, S. Moore, A. Parks, R. Barden, T. Johns, Sac. Barden and L. Brew.

Mr & Mrs Godden celebrating their Golden Wedding with their family in 1936.

Old People's Party. Celebrating are Mrs Eric Clarke, Mrs Chinnery and Mr Albert Brown in the Vestry Hall.

Mr G. Hatcher outside the stables behind Chaneys Bakery.

5th Battalion of the Buffs Territorials. I. Hickmott (big drum), H. Hinkley (side drums).

Doctor Brett, Chilworth

Duchy Chapman, who lived in Rangers Row, always had a red hand-kerchief fixed to his belt because he was hit with a pick when working for Callanders. Bill Giggles is holding the rammer and I am in the trench.

Old English Fair. I think this was in Great Swifts Park in 1922. Mr W. Winch is in the top hat.

Mr & Mrs Fisher. Mr Fisher worked for Williams and Miles, Coal Merchants. They lived in a row of cottages where Liptons now stands.

Cranbrook Operatic Society (I think).
Some of the people I recognise are Mrs Brett,
Miss Hudson, Miss Wells, Mrs Goldsmith,
Miss M. Allen and Miss Marshall.

Members of the Cranbrook Part-time A.F.S.
are: T. Harding, R. Barden, Langridge,
K. Humphrey, H. Barden, E. Smith,
H. Burgess, Field, J. Butler, S. Neave and
Relf B. Smith.

Part-time firemen during the Second World
War. Firemen from Cranbrook, Hawkhurst,
Goudhurst and Benenden A.F.S. are present.